Instituted by God

Instituted by God

*A Christian Look at Civil Government,
Politics, and Voting*

ADAM MURRELL

RESOURCE *Publications* · Eugene, Oregon

INSTITUTED BY GOD
A Christian look at Civil Government, Politics, and Voting

Resource Publications
An Imprint of Wipf and Stock Publishers
199 W. 8th Ave., Suite 3
Eugene, OR 97401
www.wipfandstock.com

ISBN 13: 978-1-62032-146-1
Manufactured in the U.S.A.

Let every person be subject to the governing authorities.
For there is no authority except from God and those
that exist have been instituted by God.

—ROMANS 13:1, ESV

Contents

Introduction

BENJAMIN FRANKLIN once remarked nothing in the world can be said to be certain except death and taxes. To that short list I think one could reasonably add another submission: change in politics. By the time you read this book, the political illustrations I have used certainly will be passé, and new political issues will take center stage. But that's okay. While the names and faces are constantly changing, the core of the issues I discuss herein remain constant. Here, for example, are a few items that are unchanging according to the Bible: the basic function of government; Christian duties and responsibilities in a free society; requirements for electing civil leaders; the ethics of voting; and even perhaps the eligibility of a candidate running for political office. These are just a few of the issues I set out to explain to voters in this short work, reminding the public that they have an awesome responsibility in their nation and a duty to approach government, politics, and voting from a biblical perspective.

This small book sets out to assist Christians in pursuing that endeavor in this year's presidential election and beyond. It is a work designed to help Christians understand why they should gladly serve America and exercise their patriotic responsibility on Election Day. However, it doesn't advocate for any one particular party since all parties evolve in belief sets at different stages and not all within the parties share monolithic ideas. What's more, this is also a book that seeks to provide an answer to the fundamental inquiry: *for whom should we vote?* I am reminded of the story in the book of Joshua where the title character has an encounter with the pre-incarnate Son of God. Joshua approaches the stranger standing before him with sword drawn, and Joshua wants to know: "Are you for us or for our enemies?" To this the man responds, "Neither; but as commander of the army of the LORD I have now come" (Josh 5:13–15).

Much like Joshua, we want to know if God is on *our* side—if he is for *our* particular political candidate. Inquiring minds want to know if Jesus would vote Democrat, Republican, or third-party. Throughout the history of this nation, many people aligned the name of Jesus with their political objectives, suggesting that God was exclusively on the side of revolution from England, slavery, prohibition, pacifism (and *vice versa*), or any other number of monumental moments. But all of these speculations about which side the divine is on miss the mark because such language about God choosing sides approaches the topic from a faulty perspective of how God operates. We are asking the wrong question.

Again we return to the story of Joshua when we are confronted with the issue of determining "God's candidate." For starters, we must properly phrase the question. Otherwise the answer will always be the one given by the pre-incarnate Jesus to the inquiry of Joshua: "Neither." Politically speaking, the Lord is neither on the side of any particular Democrat nor any specific Republican, just as he was not on the side of Joshua and the Israelites as we understand it. Jesus explained to Joshua that if he was to be victorious, he must obey the commands of the Lord. In essence, when the Israelites later proved victorious in the Battle of Jericho, it was not because God was on their side per se but because Joshua and his men were on the side of God. Likewise, we would do well to discover which candidate is on the Lord's side, so to speak—the one who most faithfully (yet imperfectly) obeys the divine commands. In this manner, we can better judge how to cast our ballot properly and according to the dictates of Scripture, ensuring we are truly on the proper side. And that, in a nutshell, is how we should focus our efforts in knowing how to vote.

Time is short, and the 2012 presidential election cycle is nearly underway, so let's begin to discover how best to view the role of government in our society and make an impactful contribution on society while voting your conscience.

1

The Function of Civil Government

CAPTURING THE mood of the American elector-
ate during his first inaugural address to the nation,
President Ronald Reagan lamented, "Government is not
the solution to our problem; government *is* the problem."[1]
This sentiment—one that is increasing notably by the day,
according to a recent Gallup survey[2]—in recent years has
spawned political movements seeking to limit, reduce, or
modify the scope of authority and power exercised by the
federal government. Citizens are growing more distrustful
of civil authorities and are mobilizing to oppose authority
rather than submit to it, serving it joyfully with a pure heart
and a clear conscience. Everything from Tea Party rallies to
the Occupy Wall Street demonstrations are clear indicators
that people at both ends of the political spectrum are fed up
with the rapid expansion of a government that nurtures a
creeping intrusion into seemingly every aspect of our lives
and fosters corruption and abuse of power.

1. The entire text of President Ronald Reagan's January 20, 1981,
Inaugural Address can be found at: http://www.reagan.utexas.edu
/archives/speeches/1981/12081a.htm.

2. Mendes, "In U. S., Fear of Big Government at Near-Record
Level."

All of this has led many to question what we should expect from our government and our elected leaders. Or more specifically, what is the proper role of government?

While that question will continue to be debated with much vigor and passion by folks of all political stripes, the Christian might do well to consider it in broader terms. That is, what is the role of civil government in a society—not merely in our own democratic republic, but in all societies? What is its primary purpose, according to the Bible? How are Christians to view secular, civil governments? Are they something to be distrustful of? Should we reject government as much as possible? These, I believe, are questions every Christian needs to wrestle with and have a firm grasp of in order to be a good citizen of his or her society—whatever form it may take.

Before I explain my own understanding of what the Bible says the role of government is in a society, let me begin by first stating four erroneous views of the role of government embraced by Christians throughout the centuries that challenge a proper understanding of Scripture.

1. GOVERNMENTS SHOULD COMPEL RELIGION

Unfortunately, this has not always been the consensus held by the church. In fact, for the majority of ecclesiastical history, the prevailing sentiment was that governments can be used as the strong arm of the church to compel certain practices. The famous fourth-century Latin theologian St. Augustine developed the concept of "just war" under some circumstances. Although initially opposed to the idea of using force to coerce his rivals, Augustine eventually sought refuge and justification for physical persuasion in the parable in which Jesus said, "Compel people to come in, that my house may be filled" (Luke 14:23). Because of the unfortunate misinterpretation of a single theologian, later Roman Catholic believers and Protestants alike used St. Augustine's "just war" principle to wage conflict against Christian dissenters during the age of the inquisition and the "wars of religion" of the sixteenth and seventeenth century. It was also used by Lutherans and Reformed against Anabaptists.

But this view has passed out of popularity with Christians as they have come to realize compelling people is inconsistent with the teachings of Jesus and the biblical understanding of the nature of salvation. Paul the apostle teaches that a person without supernatural enlightenment cannot understand the truth of God and considers it utter "foolishness" (1 Cor 2:14). No matter how hard one tries to persuade another, no matter how convincing an argument may be, and no matter how much physical pain one inflicts (or threatens to inflict) upon another, genuine conversion is not possible without divine involvement. Metaphysical truths about God and the true condition of our fallen state remain cloaked in darkness apart from supernatural intervention. Spiritual understanding takes a divine gift of grace and cannot be induced on others by force. The Spirit must first set the enslaved heart free—a heart that became in bondage as a consequence of the fall—for a person to see himself or herself for what that person truly is (John 8:34; Rom 3:9; 8:7; Eph 2:1–9). No amount of force or persuasion can change that reality. Unfortunately, it has taken the better part of human history to recognize this and to act accordingly.

2. GOVERNMENTS SHOULD BAN RELIGION

The opposite view from compulsion is the separation dogma of restriction. This idea is the view that religious beliefs and discourse should not be mixed with political discussion and should never be a factor when involved in the decision-making process of politics or governmental functions. This radical view has only become prevalent in recent decades as a consequence of an unfortunate ruling by our nation's highest court.

In 1947, in the landmark case of *Everson v. Board of Education*, the United States's Supreme Court, in a 5-4 decision, declared, "The First Amendment has erected a wall between church and state. That wall must be kept high and impregnable. We could not approve the slightest breach."[3] The phrase "separation of church and state" that was invoked by the court, a mantra that is all too common today, was taken from an exchange of private letters between President Thomas Jefferson and the Baptist Association of Danbury, Connecticut.

The Danbury Baptists sent a letter to Jefferson praising his election to office and lauding his championing of religious liberty. However, in the same letter, the Baptists expressed some grave concerns over the language in the first amendment, including its guarantee for the "free exercise of religion." What concerned them was the vague

3. A full transcript of the opinion of the court can be found at: http://caselaw.lp.findlaw.com/scripts/getcase.pl?court=us&vol=330&invol=1.

language that seemed to imply "religious privileges . . . [are] as favors granted and not as inalienable rights."[4] In short, the Danbury Baptists feared that the constitution suggested the "exercise of religion" was government-given (alienable) and not divine-given (inalienable). In other words, if the government could bestow this "right" upon the people, it could just as easily remove or suppress it.

Jefferson responded by assuring the apprehensive Baptists that the government was powerless to interfere with religious expression. He personally had no desire, intention, or power to regulate or interfere with religious practice. He, along with the ninety framers of the constitution, believed that the first amendment to the constitution was enacted only to prevent the federal government from establishing "a particular form of Christianity," something akin to the national church in England, the very abusive institution many were fighting against in Europe.

In a pithy reply to the Baptists on January 1, 1802, Jefferson merely reassured his supporters that a "wall of separation between Church and State" had been erected, prohibiting the federal government from enacting any particular protestant denomination as *the* church of America. This correct understanding of Jefferson's words, unfortunately, has been lost to most people today, with many falsely believing the constitution was written to suppress religious discourse and thought from the public arena.

In reality, the court's ruling ushered in a precipitous slide toward moral bankruptcy and anarchy as the "wall of

4. Letter of October 7, 1801, from Danbury (CT) Baptist Association to Thomas Jefferson as quoted in Barton, "The Separation of Church and State," 37–39.

separation" erected by the court has now catapulted from *freedom of religion* to *freedom from religion*. A host of un-intended outcomes have ensued. Here are a few examples of the consequences of embracing a supreme separationist perspective:

- In *District of Abington Township v. Schempp* (1963), the Supreme Court struck down voluntary Bible readings and recitation of the Lord's Prayer in public schools.

- More recently, a federal judge ordered a Texas school district to prohibit prayer at a high school graduation ceremony, a ruling that also forbids students from using specific religious words, including "prayer" and "amen."[5]

- The Tenth Circuit US Court of Appeals ruled the private Utah Highway Patrol Association can no longer pay for and erect memorial crosses for fallen heroes on state land, citing the separation clause of the constitution.[6]

- Catholic Charities of Rockford was ordered by the courts to permit homosexual couples to adopt children or to serve as foster parents since the charity receives federal funding. The organization, though, chose to close its doors rather than "contract with the state of Illinois whose laws would force us to partici-

5. Starnes, "Federal Judge Prohibits Prayer at Texas Graduation Ceremony."

6. Bohon, "Supreme Court Declines Case Banning Crosses on Utah Highways."

pate in activity offense to the moral teachings of the church."[7]

- The US Supreme Court ruled monuments displaying plaques with biblical text at two Kentucky courthouses were unconstitutional because the displays were blatantly religious.[8]

- The ACLU filed a lawsuit in Ohio to remove a decades-old granite monument of the Ten Commandments on the lawn of the Lucas County Courthouse, arguing it violated the Establishment Clause. (One has to wonder just which commandment the ACLU finds so offensive)![9]

- The congressional franking commission, a group that reviews all congressional mail, has banned US House members from writing "Merry Christmas" in any official mail.[10]

In fact, these examples underscore the bitter reality of what happens when our society embraces a perverted view of government. What began as a safeguard from the potential tyrannical despotism inherent in many cultures has morphed into a state-sponsored aggression against, most notably, the Christian religion. These illustrations all point to the inanity of divorcing religion from law and un-

7. Brachear, "Catholic Charities of Rockford Ends Foster Care, Adoption Services."

8. Reiter, "Federal Judge Says Ten Commandments Shall Stay At Courthouse."

9. Ibid.

10. Santarelli, "U. S. House Members Banned From Writing 'Merry Christmas' In Official Mail."

derscore the reality that when the foundation (e.g., religious morals) is removed from government, the entire structure crumbles.

While most Christians would decry these obvious and absurd restrictions, some professing Christians have bought into this notion of complete separation. Some wrongfully think the secular and religious do not cross over and that the two can run in parallel throughout life. This, however, is a radically dangerous mindset, one that has harmful consequences and destroys nations. Without understanding the divine moral foundation inherent in laws, the rational basis to object to evil (or at least the breakdown of morality in a society) evaporates. Consider:

- Why should marriage be restricted to a man and a woman? Why not two men or two women? Why only two people? What about folks who are in "love" with their pets?

- What's wrong with a woman terminating the fetus growing inside her body? It's her body; she can do with it whatever she wants—right?

- Why can't I engage in the recreational pursuit of mind-altering drugs in the privacy of my house? It's my body; who am I hurting?

- Then we have the United States's Senate, which voted on December 1, 2011, to approve a defense authorization bill that includes a provision that repeals the military ban on sex with animals or bestiality.[11] How would a person who denies moral underpin-

11. Winn, "Senate Approves Bill that Legalizes Sodomy and Bestiality in U. S. Military."

nings to laws argue against permitting the practice of bestiality?

The problem is that when we attempt to answer these questions without appealing to marriage as a divinely sanctioned institution, the right of life from our Creator, abusing the bodies given to us, or the depravity of unnatural acts with animals, we are abandoning the strongest arguments against these reckless activities and are allowing secularism to replace the moral foundation of societal thought. But when we reject the notion of absolutes and pretend there are no moral absolutes, anarchy fills the void. Divorcing the moral aspect of laws is not only foolhardy; it is also absolutely dangerous to the continuation of any society. Without a moral underpinning, there is no *rational* basis to contest anything—no matter how fantastically outrageous or harmful it might be. The wane of the greatest societies in human history can always be traced to a breakdown in the moral fabric of the society—bar none.

All of this brings us back to our earlier discussion regarding *Everson v. Board of Education*. In his dissenting opinion, Justice Jackson wrote the most telling statements of the ruling. Little could he have imagined just how far the country would stray from their Christian moorings when he lamented "advocating complete and uncompromising separation of Church from State, seem[s] utterly discordant."[12] The last half-century is incontrovertible evidence of what happens when religion is divorced from the civil government.

12. For web location to text of Justice Jackson's dissenting opinion, see note 3.

Indeed, Mr. Jackson. America continues to pay the price for embracing such an "utterly discordant" view of jurisprudence, of removing God's teaching about good and evil, as evidenced by the fact of America's social decomposition since then, everything ranging from an explosion in the number of illegitimate birth rates (from 5 percent to 41 percent) to abortions (fifty million since *Roe v. Wade*) to teen suicides (tripled in number) to violent crimes (soared more than 550 percent) to being the chief producer of pornography.[13] The proof, as they say, is in the pudding.

3. GOVERNMENTS ARE EVIL

According to this view, Satan and his forces have control over governments in the world. After all, the devil led Jesus up to a high place to show him all the kingdoms of the world and said to him, "I will give you all authority and splendor; it has been given to me, and I can give it to anyone I want to. If you worship me, it will all be yours" (Luke 4:6–7). The realm of governmental power, therefore, belongs to Satan. It is demonic.

Arguably the greatest concern with relying on Satan's statement to Jesus is that the Bible elsewhere calls him the "father of lies" (John 8:44). Throughout the Bible, when Satan interacts with human beings, he is *always* deceiving them, trying to get them to believe lies, beginning with his untruth in the Garden that Eve would "be like God" if she disobeyed the Lord's commands and tasted the forbidden fruit (Gen 3:1–6). So we have two choices: we believe the apostle John, who wrote that Satan is a perpetual liar, or we

13. See Buchanan, *Suicide of a Superpower*, 46–87.

believe the supposed promises of the deceiver himself. That answer is simple: Satan would have Jesus and us, if that were possible, believe he is the ruler of this world. The truth is God reigns supreme over all his creation, neither abdicating nor permitting a single renegade molecule outside of his sovereign control. "The Most High is sovereign over all kingdoms on earth and gives them to anyone he wishes and sets over them the lowliest of people" (Dan 4:17).

God rules; Satan lies. It's truly that simple.

4. CHRISTIANS HAVE MORE IMPORTANT MATTERS THAN GOVERNMENT

This fourth view takes the position that Christians should be engaged in evangelism rather than political pursuits since the former is of eternal value. People of this persuasion say, in essence, "You cannot legislate morality, so the best course of action is to change the hearts of people through evangelism and not through the political process."

Well, to some degree—yes, quite.

But let's approach this from the aspect of observing the entirety of Jesus's earthly ministry. His life work was comprised of more than merely rectifying people's spiritual life (though, granted, that is the most important). Rather, Jesus was concerned about physical needs as well, which is why he performed many miracles that included feeding hungry people and healing diseases. In a sense, healing the physical was part of the spiritual good. If we apply this to our government, social activity that we can do to bring more comfort and aid to others can be used as a bridge to teach ultimate truths about Jesus—just as he used water in

John 4 when the woman at the well was thirsty and bread in John 6 when the crowd was hungry as a way to convey eternal truths through physical means.

Governments can permit and create climates that allow churches and other organizations to benefit the society at large, or as some governments have done in countries like North Korea and Iran, they can utterly quash missionary efforts through oppressive dictatorial regimes that forbid religious expression—other than perhaps the one permitted by the state (if at all).

Perhaps we should ask any of the tens of millions of Christians throughout the world who are forced to hide their religious beliefs from their individual despotic governments lest they be punished for their convictions. Maybe we should try to ask them if they think Christians should be in government or if they should refrain from the law-making process and hope for the best. I'm confident we all know how persecuted Christians would answer that question.

Simply stated, if Christians do not enter the political arena and fight for a moral influence on society, from where will that influence come?

THREE REASONS FOR CIVIL GOVERNMENT

Having first seen what government is *not*, we now turn our attention to what the function of government *is*. Why do we even need it? It only serves to limit our freedoms, right?

The New Testament reminds us that civil government is a means ordained by God for men to rule over societies. "Everyone," the apostle Paul writes, "must submit himself to the governing authorities, for there is no authority except

that which God has established . . . he who rebels against
the authority is rebelling against what God has instituted,
and those who do so will bring judgment on themselves"
(Rom 13:1–2). Paul—a man who suffered great injustice at
the hands of civil authorities—reminds us that the origin
and institution of government is divinely ordained.

The great bishop of Hippo, St. Augustine, said the reason God ordained government, as flawed as it might be, was
because it is necessary because of evil. One of its primary
functions, then, is to *restrain human evil*. Government,
along with the church, coexists to limit evil's impact on society. Governments "are not a terror to good works, but to
evil" (Rom 13:3, NKJV).

This might be a bit counterintuitive, especially in our
society when government is generally referred to as vil-
lainous and corrupt, yet it is government's protection that
makes our freedoms possible. The reason you can worship
according to the dictates of your conscience is because the
government protects your rights from others who would
see them suppressed; the reason you can walk outside your
house is because there are laws in place that discourage your
neighbor from looting and pillaging your residence when
you are away. The reason slavery was abolished was because
Abraham Lincoln signed the Emancipation Proclamation
in 1863, thus making it illegal. Governments do not impose
legislation to force *morality on citizens*; rather, they enact
laws to legislate *against immoral practices*.

Another reason for government is to *exercise justice*.
God appoints rulers to "bear the sword" and cautions there
is "no terror for those who do right, but for those who do
wrong" (Rom 13:3). Laws are in place to protect every citi-

zen of a society from others. If there were no laws binding a society, what recourse would there be for the scores of hundreds of people harmed by Charles Manson's murderous rampage, Timothy McVeigh's egregious act of domestic terrorism, or Bernie Madoff's Ponzi scheme? What's more, without laws established, how would any of us even find peace of mind about the more rampant "petty crimes" committed daily if we were ever to fall victim to one, everything ranging from breaking and entering to trespassing to identify theft to disturbing the peace? We all possess that inner knowledge that demands justice be paid for offenses committed against us. The next time someone does something injurious to you, just remember that justice can be exacted in this life because God ordained a civil institution to carry out justice now—and aren't you glad for it?

A third function of government is to *uphold the sanctity of life and to maintain property*. This necessarily includes life that is most fragile, regardless of one's age, whether it is at the moment of conception or in the final days of one's life. All life is sacred and holy to God, and the Lord provides us with armies and protection against foreign invaders as well as invasions from within our own society. Our *Declaration of Independence* expressed it succinctly when it uttered biblical truths that all people share an inalienable right—one bestowed by our Creator—to *life*. Government is to uphold this divine right to which every created being is entitled since, after all, our ongoing existence is a direct result of the staying power of God. "All the days ordained for me were written in your book before one of them came to be" (Ps 139:16).

Because of these integral roles government plays in our life, and because God ordains every government, Christians, first and foremost, are to respect the institution under which they are living. They are to be model citizens to the government to which they are subject, provided the government is not requiring them to sin or act contrary to God's revealed laws. In those instances, not only should Christians disobey the civil magistrates, but they are also required to do so, just as Daniel was justified when he refused to obey King Darius's decree that forbade praying to Yahweh (Dan 6). Nonetheless, our duty to civil government is really twofold: one, to be submissive and obey the laws established by the government, and two, to pray for our leaders "and all those in authority, that we may live peaceful and quiet lives in all godliness and holiness" (1 Tim 2:2). We are not merely to complain about the evil in our governments and live passively, waiting for the day when our leaders will pass out of office. Instead, we are commanded to be active in reminding them how God ordained them for protection and not to tyrannize the masses. We are to remember our leaders and recognize they are in place by the decree of God. Therefore, we are to make "requests, prayers, intercession and thanksgiving" for our leaders (1 Tim 2:1).

However bad we think our current government is, we must always remember that even a corrupt government is better than no government at all.

2

Give to Caesar What Is Caesar's

ELECTING *NOT* to vote—that's what the church group called it. Perhaps you have heard the story—or one similar—of a church whose members thought it was against God's will to vote in political elections. This community of Christians was so concerned about the prospect of a corrupt politician winning the election that they gathered prior to the election for an all-night prayer vigil. The next morning, however, they refused to vote, and the Christian candidate lost the race by a slim margin—by fewer votes than the number of people at the prayer vigil, in fact. The community of concerned believers ironically thought their prayers would be sufficient and were unaware, seemingly, that God uses human means to achieve certain ends. Their actions, or rather inactions, ensured the very thing they desperately hoped would not happen—the election of a corrupt politician.

But politics is dirty and messy; it is a crooked business. We are not supposed to be "of the world" because our true citizenship resides in heaven. Moreover, our duty is to obey God's commands and not become encumbered in the temporal affairs of civil government, right?

Well, not quite.

In fact, part of our divinely sanctioned duties is to obey the earthly structures appointed over us. Jesus said, "Give to Caesar what is Caesar's and to God what is God's" (Mark 12:17). What this means is that we are to give whatever it is our responsibility to give to the state. In our case, dwelling in a democracy (or a *democratic republic,* to be more precise), this certainly includes at a minimum that we should cast a vote for righteousness.

God gives Christians citizens in a democracy the opportunity to vote for candidates and policies that are most consistent with biblical values. We have an opportunity to cultivate a culture that recognizes the reality of the divine and to progress that biblically-minded society toward stewarding the nation forward (besides, if we don't, who will?). I am not advocating a Christian theocracy here but simply a nation whose leaders and policies promote the basic precepts of the Bible about loving one's neighbor, the sacredness of life, protection from evil, ensuring justice, equality, and religious freedom—in short, the precepts encapsulated in our nation's founding documents. Being a good steward, then, includes at the very least Christians who are well-informed enough about issues to vote intelligently for maintaining the kind of culture that is consistent with sacred Scripture.

If we do not care enough to vote for righteous candidates, then we are in essence not exercising our privilege the "kingdom of Caesar" affords to prevent widespread corruption. Yet we are called to stand against evil. St. Augustine rightly remarked that citizens of God's kingdom are best suited to be citizens of man's kingdom. And it will be those Christians citizens—or at least those influenced by Christian ethics—who put a stop to evil practices.

Remember, it is Christian citizens and the presuppositions of the Christian religion that give a *rational* basis to objective morality—something, for instance, that eventually led to the condemnation of selling Africans as property in the antebellum South and stopped the immoral practice altogether. Going further, it is Christian ethics and principles that find redemption from the tyranny of evil atheistic and secular humanistic leaders such as Lenin, Hitler, Stalin, and Pol Pot. While the atheism of these aforementioned men does not always or necessarily lead to abusing other people, it is, nevertheless, an insufficient basis for condemning the practice; only Christianity can rationally oppose it, and it is because of Christianity that objections to evil are even possible.

As well, Christian involvement in civil matters led to and continues to play a vital role in society. Throughout the ages, Christians in government have given us such things as hospitals, women's equality, capitalism, public education, respect for human life, and so much more.[1] When we elect Christians to office who have biblically based worldviews, we see the fruits of those godly men and women who apply

---

1. That said, this is not to suggest only Christians have morality, nor is it meant to imply non-Christians do not engage in humanitarian acts. Rather, it is simply to point out is that given the starting point of Christianity, these good things logically follow. Conversely, given the presupposition of, for instance, atheism, what compels atheists to show respect for their fellow human beings? How does this philanthropy logically follow from their Neo-Darwinian naturalistic premise? Simply stated, Christianity is good for society because it brings benefits to all members of society, because of the foundation which *requires* its adherents to act like the Good Samaritan. The same cannot be said for atheism.

God's principles to the troubles of the world to bring solutions to citizens of this country and abroad.

Our responsibility is the same one our forefathers captured in the 1606 charter for the first permanent English settlement in the New World called Jamestown. That initial charter spoke of the settlers' responsibility of "propagating the Christian religion."[2] The people of Jamestown understood what it would take to make that happen, and they understood part of succeeding in that stated goal was the election of Christian folks to public office who would help in ensuring religious freedom and liberty assisted in that endeavor (though not imposed upon others). Just the same, propagating the Christian religion remains our task today, but it will take voting for Christians seeking public office to ensure biblically based laws are enacted; it will take voting for principled leaders to ensure the Jamestown vision continues today. Voting is part of our great high calling to ensure we do everything humanly possible to advance the good news, including voting for people who share the same vision.

Should Christians vote in elections? Not only should they, but they must to see the best possible nation for our children and grandchildren. An ancient proverb says, "A good person leaves an inheritance for their children's children" (Prov 13:22). One of the best things any one of us could bequeath later generations is a nation whose laws are grounded in biblical truths. Who will ensure this happens if all Christians throughout America thought like that church

2. The entire text of the First Charter of Virginia, April 10, 1606, can be found at: http://avalon.law.yale.edu/17th_century/va01.asp.

group who only prayed and refused to follow it up with action?

If Christians stand idly on the wayside, they should not be surprised to wake up one morning and discover the freedoms they thought were inalienable were usurped by the very same corrupt politicians they fear so greatly. Though we are called not to be too involved in this world that we neglect our heavenly homes, our wholesale removal from the affairs of this world will only spell disaster for future generations. Our founding fathers implicitly understand the inherent wickedness of the human heart and sought to put in place checks and balances to prevent the abuse of power and the usurpation of individual freedom and liberty. But if Christians are not careful and do not follow all of Christ's commands and vote for the proper leaders, they will pay the price for their apathy, indifference, or ignorance.

Electing *not* to vote as a general principle stands in opposition to Christ's command: "Give to Caesar what is Caesar's." Caesar asks for our vote; we are to oblige him.

3

Biblical Principles for Leaders

THREE DAYS had passed, and he was just as affronted by the remarks as he was when he first heard the man utter the slanderous words. Representative Preston Brooks of South Carolina was stewing over Senator Charles Sumner's "Crimes against Kansas" speech on the senate floor in which the latter railed against the senator from Illinois and also the senator from South Carolina. Senator Sumner's inflammatory speech mocked the senator from South Carolina as a man of chivalry and accused him of taking "a mistress . . . the harlot, Slavery."[1]

It was May 1856, and the country was on a collision course with a tumultuous civil war. The issue of slavery was rearing its ugly head once again, this time over the explosive issue of whether Kansas should be admitted to the Union as a free state or as a slave state. Senator Sumner was adamant that slavery was an abomination, hence his speech on the senate floor just three days prior.

Now, on May 22, even though Representative Brooks was not personally attacked by Sumner in his speech,

1. See, "The Caning of Senator Charles Sumner" on the United States Senate website at http://www.senate.gov/artandhistory/history/minute/The_Caning_of_Senator_Charles_Sumner.htm.

his South Carolinian kinsman was. That was enough for Brooks. He headed for the Senate and entered the old chamber, where he found Sumner working busily on attaching a hand stamp to copies of his speech. Brooks approached the unsuspecting senator, metal-topped cane in hand, and slammed his weapon of choice repeatedly into the head of his political foe. Stunned onlookers were paralyzed by the scene. The wounded senator, bleeding profusely from the repeated blows, staggered about, blindly lurching about the chamber and failing to protect himself. After a minute of rage, Representative Brooks walked calmly out of the chamber, an instant hero to many in the South.

Witnessing a scene like this unfold in our day would be almost unheard of, though the verbal assaults from our politicians are at times no less venomous or hate-filled. When we elect folks to office, we generally expect a greater sense of conduct of character. Character truly does matter. Our elected representatives are supposed to be held to a higher standard to prevent such reckless and unbridled attacks as the one that transpired on the floor of the Senate chamber. It would be nice to think they are all people of unimpeachable character and that something like the assault on Senator Sumner would never happen.

But that's not reality.

Bad people run for elected office all the time. Sometimes they get elected; sometimes they don't. It is part of our responsibility to investigate who these people are, make ourselves informed voters, and vote responsibility for the right person for the job. Granted, there are countless ways to determine if someone is a suitable fit for the position, but one of the surest signs is see how the candidate matches up using the Bible as a source to determine the nature of leaders.

The apostles were chiefly concerned with local church-es determining leaders for each of their churches if the in-dividuals met certain criteria. I believe if Christians were to follow the same pattern the New Testament churches used in determining their leaders, they would almost always vote for the right person for the job. Following are a few charac-teristics the Bible required of church leaders. They are solid character traits that should define every politician if he or she desires to rule in government over others. That is, every candidate seeking the vote of a Christian should be able to pass an "elder test," a basic list of characteristics the early church used to ensure a candidate was suitable to lead.

- *Biblical leaders are to be servants* (2 Tim 2:24). It is easy to rise to a position of prominence and get a sense certain work is beneath an individual. Jesus, how-ever, showed us the true model when he washed the feet of his disciples. He did not lord his position over others but became a servant to humanity. Likewise, our elected leaders should be people to recognize the fundamental distinction between a representative *of the people* versus a representative *over the people*. Far too many fall into the latter category.

- *Biblical leaders are shepherds* (Acts 20:28). Part and parcel of the shepherd's responsibility is to care for, feed, and nurture the flock. A shepherd protects the innocent and vulnerable sheep from ravenous beasts and leads the flock to green pastures, ensuring they are adequately fed. Our leaders must protect us from the evils of this world and implement policies that ensure innocent life is protected and preserved at all stages of life. This includes protecting the unborn, all citizens against domestic and foreign attacks, and the elderly against so-called assisted suicides or euthanasia.

- *Biblical leaders are teachers* (1 Tim 3:2). Just as an elder in a church is required to be able to communicate rational, biblical truths to others, civil servants in office must also demonstrate the ability to present a coherent, biblically supported agenda for its citizens. Leadership includes understanding the basics and presenting that to the people so they can clearly rally behind that person who seeks to pursue wholesome agendas.

- *Biblical leaders are to be good stewards* (Titus 1:7a). Stewardship refers to the administration of duties or goods in a person's care. As created beings of God, we are obliged to be stewards of all aspects of life that have been entrusted to us for our use. We are not owners but trustees, managing God's goods and estates, since he is the one and original owner of all things. In the execution of stewardship, Scripture teaches us that we are to be faithful and wise, not turning entrustments into self-indulgent pursuits. Likewise, elected officials, those who are entrusted with our taxes are to use them wisely for the good of all society, are not to use the money foolishly and perversely. Worthy leaders recognize voting for fanciful schemes and creating a sea of debt for the sake of social programs to buy votes or to pander to a certain segment of society is the height of folly.

- *Biblical leaders are not to be greedy for gain* (Titus 1:7b). Along with being faithful with other people's money is the idea that one does not have an unhealthy pursuit of personal, selfish gain. Leaders are not installed for their own private benefit but to ensure the benefit of all society. What's more, a leader whose chief desire is personal gain will compromise his or her principles in that selfish pursuit of gaining more.

- *Biblical leaders discipline when necessary* (Acts 5:3; Titus 1:13). Leaders must have the courage to confront evil when necessary, wherever they may find it. All too often politicians cover for each other if misconduct is discovered within their own ranks. They make excuses for bad behavior. True leadership, however, speaks up. A true leader confronts evil in his or her one political party, domestically, or abroad and seeks to correct it.

- *Biblical leaders imitate Christ* (1 Cor 11:1). One does not have be a Christian to appreciate the flawlessness of Jesus's life and testimony. Christ was a man who preached grace, love, mercy, kindness, charity, selflessness, hospitality, equality, obedience, and virtue—characteristics that all humanity deems good. Leaders will never get the entirety of these qualities perfect as Jesus did, but they must continually strive to imitate Christ.

Scripture understands why leaders must possess these essential godly characteristics. The reason for such requirements—and the same reason Christians should insist upon them in their candidates—is that bad roots always corrupt the tree and yields bad fruit (Matt 7:15–20; Luke 6:43–45). American founding father Samuel Adams argued nothing is more essential to the proper functioning of government than entrusting power to individuals of exceptional character. He argued that a politician's private life directly influences the public.

It's not that difficult to find examples of egregious laws or practices that came about as the consequence of political leadership's deficiency in character. Whether we look to examples in foreign governments of engaging in pogroms against European Jews and banishing Christians to the gulags or to the domestic policies of politicians who actively seeking to normalize homosexuality and bestiality, we are confronted with the natural outworking of putting people in a position of power who have no scriptural moorings. The ancient Proverb rings true: "When the righteous thrive, the people rejoice; when the wicked rule, the people groan" (Prov 29:2).

America must be a nation whose leaders fear the Lord and obey his commands. For the Christian voter, there is no choice about it—character matters, both private and public. The one who strives to live his or her life in accordance with biblical precepts is the one who merits our vote, because morality is essential for leaders to ensure they are more likely to do the right thing when confronted with overwhelming opportunities daily to act contrary to divine laws.

4

Single-Issue Voting

IN 2004, before he became Pope Benedict XVI, Cardinal Joseph Ratzinger, then head of the Vatican's Congregation for the Doctrine of Faith, gave single-issue thinking some wriggle room when it comes to the topic of abortion. Voting for a pro-abortion candidate is a practice officially forbidden by the Roman Catholic Church. In a memo to the cardinal of Washington DC, however, Ratzinger qualified the church's position to permit faithful Catholics the opportunity to vote for a pro-abortion candidate. In the memo, he reasoned that one may vote for a candidate who supports abortion rights provided: (1) abortion is not the primary reason for one's vote, and (2) if the candidate has other positions that outweigh the abortion issue.[1]

If you find yourself scratching your head, you're probably not alone. It's hard for me to imagine a proportionate reason to justify the favoring of taking of an innocent human life. What outweighs the protection of life? Is there something more valuable than defending the pinnacle of God's creation—human life?

1. Cardinal Ratzinger's memorandum was originally published online July 3, 2004, by the Italian magazine *L'Espresso*. See Thavis, "Cardinal Ratzinger Lays Out Principles On Denying Communion, Voting" for a Roman Catholic perspective.

The Vatican's (okay, let's just call it what it is) politically motivated memo, which was designed to assuage a certain portion of its practitioners, is in essence saying single-issue voting is neither necessary nor wise. Otherwise, why else would the magisterium give its approval for people to vote for pro-abortion candidates? The problem, though, comes when we start to consider other single-issue policies, other issues that every rational person would agree should disqualify a person from public office. For instance, a candidate who advocated the widespread use of blackmail as a form of government efficiency would be deemed incompetent, regardless of his or her political platform. A person who endorsed racial or gender discrimination would be disqualified regardless of his or her other views. A candidate who suggested pedophilia should not be a crime—that stance alone would end that person's political career. The list could go on and on. The idea is simply to point out that every single person has *at least* a single issue in mind that would, to that person, disqualify a candidate from political leadership.

It's the same with work. Suppose you were interviewing potential candidates for a certain job—let's say baking in a bakery in your downtown store—and the interviewee informed you he will not work before 8:00 a.m. However, you need him at the store well before that hour to prepare the breads, pastries, cupcakes, croissants, doughnuts, and pies. What if a potential bank teller informed you she did not like people and did not want to provide cheerful service? That single issue would most likely be enough for you not to hire that person.

Politics is no different. Every voter must decide what those issues are; one must choose which issues are deal-breakers. Many evangelicals believe there is no other issue where the stakes are so high or the moral contrast is so striking. I cannot fathom a more-telling example of lapse in moral judgment than to the politician who endorses the "right" to kill an unborn child—or infanticide, if we were to stop using Orwellian language and were honest. The utter inability to see evil and oppose it at all costs should disqualify someone from public office as much as any candidate who would endorse racism, bigotry, discrimination, fraud, bribery, or blackmail. The irony, however, is that a pro-abortion position is treated as a form of societal progression, but the killing of a child is far more heinous than any of the others listed.

The starting point for Christians on the issue of life must be the strong and consistent testimony in support of the divine gift of life from the pages of Scripture. Even the unborn child is dear and precious to the Lord, as the psalmist testified: "For you created my inmost being; you knit me together in my mother's womb. I praise you because I am fearfully and wonderfully made; your works are wonderful, I know that full well" (Ps 139:13–14). Unborn babies are more than merely "masses of tissue" or "bags of protoplasm." They are specific acts of creation that, at the moment of conception, have unique human genetic codes and within a few weeks, have beating hearts, brain waves, sensitivity to pain, and thumbs to suck. The humanness of unborn babies is evident as, for example, when John the Baptist leaped in his mother's womb at the sound of Mary's voice (Luke 1:41). Are we seriously going to deny the personhood of John the Baptist in the womb—or any unborn child, for that matter?

Another telling passage that strips away any potential confusion is found in Exodus 21:22–25: "If people are fighting and hit a pregnant woman and she gives birth prematurely but there is no serious injury, the offender must be fined whatever the woman's husband demands and the court allows. But if there is serious injury, you are to take life for life, eye for eye, tooth for tooth, hand for hand, foot for foot, burn for burn, wound for wound, bruise for bruise."

While commentators differ regarding whether this passage refers only to a miscarriage or to a live but premature birth (because the Hebrew verb *yasa*, "to come out," is always used in the Bible to refer to live births), the thrust of the message is clear: an unborn child is a *nephesh*, a soul, a living human being nurtured in the womb.[2] Premature births resulting in death carry a death penalty for either the mother or the child, a hefty sentence that would not be imposed if the unborn child were not a living being.

Taking the life of a child in the womb, according to the testimony of Scripture, is a serious offense that, under the Old Testament Laws of Moses, carried grave consequences. Life is deemed sacred because of the Creator, and humanity is called to honor and protect it as such. Yet, ironically, our society does not place the same intrinsic value on life as does Scripture. In fact, animals carry more rights and protection than the unborn. Just in my home state, current as of the time of writing this, Virginia Statutes § 3.2-6500–6590 and § 18.2-361 prohibit cruelty to animals. One has to wonder

2. For a detailed study of abortion and Scripture, see White, "An Eye for an Eye? Exodus and Abortion."

why it could be a felony to "beat, maim, mutilate, or kill any animal," while at the same time it is permissible to mutilate or kill an unborn child with a beating heart in the name of "reproductive rights." Could we at the very least not change the laws to reflect a fetus as being of equal worth to that of an animal? Are not unborn children at least as valuable as your household pet?

All the politically correct language in the world will not change the reality that abortion is infanticide, and it is an abomination to take the very life created by God. The ancient Hebrews were to have nothing to do with killing the unborn, and neither should we. For this very reason, and on this particular issue, I am a convinced single-issue voter. I believe life trumps all other issues, and any candidate who refuses to protect the most defenseless of all God's creation will not have my support. I think it is safe to say that no Christian would knowingly vote for a candidate whose platform is the widespread persecution of Christ-followers, so I find it curious when I discover professing believers who have no qualms about voting for a candidate whose platform is the wide-spread persecution of the unborn. (That said, one could argue that, in rare circumstances, given a choice between two pro-choice candidates, the lesser of two evils should be supported).

The only way to reverse this trend is to change the hearts of the American people. Merely passing laws will not prevent abortions from taking place; only a heart longing to obey the Lord will. The church and every professing Christian must cultivate a culture of life from the youngest child to the oldest adult. Abortion remains a great stain on this nation, just as genocide of the Jews is a blotch on

Germany's past. The only way to combat evil is to recognize it, confront it, and defeat it entirely. We start that process by voting for good people who will do the right thing, who will move to protect all human life.

Sometimes people ask, "How would Jesus vote?" While that question might not always have a simple answer, I think it's say to say that Jesus would not vote in violation of his own divine laws and would surely cast a vote for life. Abortion is a toxin polluting the moral fabric of our society. Let's emulate Jesus and do the same.

ADDITIONAL SINGLE-ISSUE POLITICS

While the issue of life remains for many people (on both sides of the issue) a single-issue decider, I submit the Christian could make a compelling case for at least three other paramount issues: promotion of family values, fiscal responsibility, and defense of the country. Let's look briefly at each of the three separately.

Promotion of family values. For any society to survive, let alone thrive, strong families must be at its core. I am reminded of the story of a father who gave each of his children a stick and asked them to break it in half. They each do so easily. Then the father gathered all the broken sticks, bound them together, and asked the children to break the bundle of sticks. None of them could, of course. The message of the story, quite naturally, is that when families stick together—fathers and mothers lovingly providing for, giving of themselves to, and instilling morality in their children—the family is much stronger because each person within that individual community is more secure. This, in turn, is the foundation on which the society at large is built—strong families coalescing to build strong societies.[3]

But what happens when politicians are not convinced the traditional family is the best or only form of family? What happens when elected leaders promote a planned destruction of the family as every society has known since the beginning of mankind? We have been told, for instance, by politicians at all levels of public office up to and including the current president of the United States that it is time "we as a nation finally recognize relationships between two men or two women [are] just as real and admirable as relationships between a man and a woman."[4]

Aside from the breathtaking audacity of such a statement (not to mention the biological and physiological absurdity of it), the idea by some is that marriage is merely self-centered sex. Reducing marriage and family to this level is simply tragic. Biblical marriage includes *a man* and *a woman* coming together and multiplying (Gen 1:28). Marriage and family is also a small community in which God and godliness are taught and where instruction is given as the basis of one's living (Gen 18:18–19; Deut 4:9; 6:6–8; 11:18–21; Prov 1:8; 6:20; 22:6). Society has an interest in seeing strong religious families, as the future of society is dependent upon marriages that produce offspring, instill industriousness in their children, and teach them to obey

3. For a thoughtful book emphasizing the central role of the family in achieving the common good, see Santorum, *It Takes a Family*.

4. For a video and audio transcript of the president's speech, see *U. S. News & World Report* article, "Is Obama Having It Both Ways on Gay Marriage?" at: http://www.usnews.com/news/blogs/god-and-country/2009/10/15/is-obama-having-it-both-ways-on-gay-marriage.

authority. When the family crumbles, the inevitable result is always that societies are not far behind.

Fiscal responsibility. When we begin with the premise that all things belong to God and we are commanded in Scripture to be good stewards of the resources he has entrusted to each and every one of us, it naturally flows that our elected leaders are likewise required to be responsible with the resources they have been entrusted. Financial prudence does not stop at the doorstep of family homes. It belongs in the halls of government as well. "The wise have wealth and luxury, but fools spend whatever they get" (Prov 21:20, NLT). Informed voters must decide if our leaders are using our taxes for the biblically supported common good of society or if the policies and spending bills are tools of financial orgies of greed. No one in his or her right mind would allow the infamous scam artist Bernie Madoff to manage his or her money, so why would any sane person entrust his or her tax dollars to folks who are just as reckless, wasteful, and distrustful as the Ponzi-scheme billionaire?

Defense of the nation. Picture this scene in your mind. You come home late at night after a long day at work only to find your house had been invaded by thieves. Your wife and children have been beaten and gagged. They lie semiconscious in the corner from the attack. You are tired and beaten down emotionally and psychologically from the pressures of work. You shrug your shoulders and walk upstairs to your room, calling to the intruders to take whatever they want; just don't do any further harm to your family.

As absurd as this story is, we all recognize the utter failing of the man to protect his family. Who among us would praise this guy or think it is acceptable not to defend his family? He failed at the most basic level to provide protection for those under his care.

Government has a similar responsibility. Politicians have in their charge the entire society and are responsible for protecting them from abusers and those who seek to inflict harm, foreign or domestic. We as citizens have a right to expect this of our government. Not only do we anticipate physical protection from foreign invaders or domestic terrorists, but we also insist the civil authorities to use their power to ensure religious freedom is preserved and also that they do not promote or entrench certain kinds of evil. The government is to render services to its citizens but must not be a force for evil. Voters, then, must do everything in their power to ensure the latter does not happen.

Again I repeat: we are all single-issue voters on some things. Each of us must determine for ourselves what those issues are and vote accordingly. That said, while many political convictions will vary from Christian to Christian, it is not as if God leaves all issues up to our own subjectivity. He has spoken clearly in Scripture on many issues, and we are responsible to obey his revealed will. On some matters, there is no negotiating. Therefore, the issues before each and every one of us are: do we care enough to listen to his commands, and are we willing to be consistent Christians and obey his instruction?

Being an informed voter is part of our daily walk. Let's take our responsibility seriously and vote with biblical principles. That will truly be for the benefit of society.

5

Jesus Is Not on the Ballot

A s OF the time of writing this chapter, the Republican presidential candidates are but a few weeks away from the all-important first-in-the-nation Iowa caucuses, the first step in securing the presidential nomination on the road to the White House. But there is one candidate who is having trouble courting some evangelical voters, experiencing the same dilemma as he suffered four years ago when he ran for the nation's highest office in Iowa. The man's name is Mitt Romney, and one of the reasons he is having trouble garnering support is because of his religious beliefs. Romney, you see, is a practicing Mormon. Even after four years of trying to woo middle-America supporters, Romney's "Mormon problem" simply won't go away.

Iowa political director for former Speaker of the House and presidential candidate Newt Gringrich, Craig Bergman, told a McClatchy Newspaper focus group that "a lot of evangelicals believe God would give us four more years of Obama just for the opportunity to expose the cult of Mormon."[1]

1. Powers, "Mitt Romney's Mormon Problem in the Iowa Caucuses Simply Won't Die," 2–4.

Bergman's comments do not seem to be that far removed from reality (yet, ironically, he was fired the following day for his assessment).

The Ethics and Public Policy Center has been studying this very issue and reports a large number of voters "refuse to vote for a Mormon."[2] And the Pew Forum on Religion & Public Life pointed out in a recent poll there are "really high negatives for Romney among white evangelicals"[3] because of his religion. David Lane of Iowa's Pastors and Pews—an evangelical who is instrumental in mobilizing like-minded Christians—said bluntly, "Eighty percent of evangelicals will not vote for Romney in a contested primary, and 20 to 30 percent will stay home or go third party in the general election because of the Mormon issue."[4]

There are others who lament the other imperfect candidate, Newt Gingrich, who is currently on his third marriage and publicly admitted to an extramarital affair during his tenure in the 1990s as Speaker of the House. Conservative evangelicals openly wonder how they can cast a vote for someone who has had multiple wives.

But are these legitimate concerns that are troubling enough to disqualify someone from the nation's highest elected office? Are evangelicals prohibited from voting for Romney because of his religious views? Should evangelicals not vote for Gingrich because of marital infidelity? Should Christians only vote for . . . the perfect candidate?

I say no, and here is why: for starters, King David.

2. Ibid., 12.
3. Ibid., 17–18.
4. Ibid., 26–29.

David was an extraordinary man gifted by God whose life included a number of highs and lows. He was single-mindedly committed to Yahweh, an author of sacred Scripture, and a man after the Lord's own heart (1 Sam 13:14). Yet despite all of these positive qualities, David was guilty of some of the most flagrant and egregious sins in the Bible, including adultery and murder. Fortunately for David—and for the rest of us, for that matter—the Bible does not do away with morally compromised people. For another example, consider the life of the apostle Paul (formerly, Saul of Tarsus), the chief of all sinners (1 Tim 1:15). Here was a man whose life's work and mission included the zealous persecution and murder of Christ-followers, yet his life was transformed and he even became an author of two-thirds of the New Testament. Not only this, but his newfound zeal for Christ following his conversion also resulted in the establishment of countless churches throughout Europe and Asia. So does God give up on sinners and limit what they are qualified to do because of personal transgressions? Absolutely not. So our attitudes as well should not be that of one that seeks to limit or disparage others for past, repentant sins. The message and good news that Christianity carries is redemption and restoration for those who repent.

But what about someone who does not believe in the God of the Bible? Can we vote for someone who is a non-Christian?

To begin with, I believe it is good to proceed cautiously through this issue since none of the Bible's authors lived in a society like the one we now enjoy. However, we can use Scripture, as much as practical, to address this question, even though there is no explicit command or example to follow. That said, I believe there is some scriptural warrant for Christians to vote for the individual who upholds policies that will be for the societal good—*good* as defined by the Bible, of course. This divinely structured "common good" presumably includes adhering to laws and policies that reflect the righteousness, love, and justice of God. With this in mind, it would seem that Scripture provides us with principles by which we are able to evaluate candidates and their role in providing justice for citizens under their realm of influence. Here, then, are seven ways in which justice is to be achieved personally and through the state:[5]

- *Love of neighbors.* Christ commands us to love our neighbors as ourselves. Our neighbors, according to Jesus, include all those who likewise are fashioned in the image of God. We are to love all mankind and are to treat everyone as our neighbor (Luke 10:27–37).

- *Help others in need.* Everything we possess is on loan from God. He shares with us temporal blessings so we, in gracious love, will help the less fortunate, feed the hungry, clothe the naked, and comfort the weary (Matt 25:31–46). Both church and state play a role in accomplishing that end.

- *Exercise righteous judgment and ensure justice is served.* As mentioned previously, the civil government is to ensure righteousness prevails, and the Old

5. My starting point was borrowed from Francis J. Beckwith, who offers four points in which Scripture instructs the individual and the state to do justice. See his, "Is It Permissible for a Christian to Vote for a Mormon?"

Testament is just as adamant with calls for justice and condemnations of injustice directed to the state (Deut 24:19–22; Prov 31:8–9; Isa 58:6–10).

- *Ensure religious expression prevails.* King Darius in Daniel 6 serves as a striking example of what to do and what *not* to do. He should be applauded for having Daniel as one of his administrators, but he was wrong for surrounding himself with foolish advisors who eventually convinced him to pass laws suppressing religious expression and condemning Daniel to the lion's den. The lesson here is that everyone one of us must surround ourselves with wise friends and advisors so we do not make similar foolish choices. Politically speaking, presidents have this power through appointing God-fearing judges to courts who will uphold Judeo-Christian principles and not seek—like so many secular activist judges of today—to overthrow religious freedom as Darius's advisors tried to do centuries ago.

- *Be financially responsible.* The Proverbs are filled with advice regarding the wisdom of working diligently and saving compared with laziness and reckless spending (Prov 6:6–8; 10:4; 13:11; 21:5; 24:3–4; etc.). Our elected leaders have a moral responsibility to their citizens to use resources wisely, just as we are responsible to God to use the money that he has entrusted to us prudently (Matt 25:14–30; Rom 12:5–8).

- *Exercise dominion over God's resourceful earth.* The Lord placed Adam and Eve in the Garden and charged them with ruling over the entirety of his creation (Gen 1:26). All resources and materials in the earth were deliberately placed there by God to provide shelter, food, medicine, and other advancements we discover daily to improve living conditions around the world. Part of exercising dominion includes the responsibility to maintain the integrity of the earth (Adam and Eve were required to work the Garden before the fall) and help other nations utilize their natural resources to benefit their citizens as well.

- *Obey the commands of God for an orderly society.* The Ten Commandments—a summation of the moral law—contain, in addition to our duty toward God, our duty toward each other. What this essentially says to us is that there is a right way and a wrong to function in a society. The Lord outlined the basic social fabric for civilizations that we must esteem and maintain. In political terms, this means respecting the sanctity of life, traditional marriage, family values, honesty, and the rule of law.

The candidate who embraces these principles and strives to maintain them is the leader whose behavior the Bible supports, even if that person is not a believing Christian. So can a believer in good conscience vote for a candidate who is not a practicing Christian? I believe it is permissible for a Christian to vote for someone who will uphold the dignity of all life, respect the divine institution of marriage, promote Christian values, exercise fiscal restraint, and appoint biblically minded men and women to serve as just judges. In fact, I would go beyond merely suggesting it is permissible and argue that it is our duty to vote for someone who will champion these fundamental truths. When we elect the president into public office, we are not casting a vote for Theologian-in-Chief but rather for Commander-in-Chief.

Our overriding concern should be for the advancement of the common good of the society, and that necessarily entails someone who will uphold and advance Christian ethics and principles. Whether that individual truly understands what he or she is doing or the true reason behind his or her worldview is an entirely different issue altogether. As long as Christ's commands are obeyed and carried forth, we can in good conscience know a vote for biblical principles is a vote for righteousness. And in that, Christians should take comfort.

6

A Motherhood Debate

REACTION TO the designation of former Alaskan
Governor Sarah Palin as the Republican nominee for
vice president in 2008 was wide and varied. Some praised
her voting record while others loathed her conservative
ideology; some lauded the idea of a woman as the vice president while still others detested the fact Palin is pro-life. A
few were outspoken critics that a wife and a mother would
pursue political office, yet the majority viewed her selection
as breaking through the proverbial glass ceiling.

So how should evangelicals view Sarah Palin, or any
women in public office? Does Palin, among other females
in politics, present a dilemma for complementarians (folks
who believe the Bible teaches male and female—though created by God with equal dignity, worth, value, and essence—
each have distinct roles whereby the male is responsible for
lovingly exercising authority over his wife and the female
is to offer willing submission and help to her husband)?
Perhaps more importantly, though, does the Bible prohibit
women from seeking public office or working outside the
home? How are Christians to think biblically about this
issue?

I submit that from the outset of this discussion, we must bear in mind—as I have mentioned in an earlier chapter—that the president is not Theologian-in-Chief but Commander-in-Chief. We are not seeking a spiritual head to feed us spiritual truths as elders inside the organized church are required to do (John 21:17; 1 Tim 3:1–13; Titus 1:5–9). And quite frankly, the president is not held to the same moral standard as an elder is, though having a professing Christian in elected office is without question a tremendous advantage and blessing. While we can look to our spiritual leaders as the model we would want our candidates to emulate, we must not impose upon politicians the same standard; we must be careful not to apply the criteria for church on the kingdom of this world. The Bible does not require that, so neither should we.

But this appeal has not stopped some evangelicals from taking the paradigm of the church and home and applying it to the secular. This, I believe, is the unintentional mistake by people seeking to be thoroughly biblical. In so doing, they make the mistake of going beyond the teaching of Scripture and making dogmatic applications where God chose to remain silent (especially given the fact we live in a democratic republic and not a Christian theocracy).

In fact, the Bible does mention on occasion women who were called to specific roles outside the normal, specific roles given to them in the church and home. The author of 1 Kings 10:1–13 portrays the Queen of Sheba favorably when he notes her meeting with King Solomon; Queen Esther was specifically raised up as an example of a godly woman who appropriately exerted influence for the good of her people (Esth 2:17); and Deborah was chosen to lead Israel as a judge and prophetess and played a crucial role in leading the Israelites into battle and securing forty years of peace (Judg 4–5). In light of these positive examples from Scripture, it is difficult to say categorically that women such as Lady Jane Grey, Queen Elizabeth, Queen Victoria, Margaret Thatcher, or Goldie Maier were violating biblical principles because they simply were born with the wrong set of chromosomes. I think it is a stretch to condemn women from seeking office for the sole reason that they are women.

Having said that, however, and with the full understanding that the Bible is silent regarding any supposed gender restriction from secular office, the question Christians must consider is if it is *wise* for a specific woman in a specific time in her life to seek public office (and of course, we can and should ask the same question for any man as well).[1] Needless to say, every situation is unique, and every situation would have to be evaluated separately. For instance, the answer for a female candidate seeking public office would invariably differ from that of a single woman to someone in her fifties with no children in the home to one who is married with six young children in the home, with the youngest suffering from a genetic abnormality. The answer to the question would undoubtedly be different in each of the given situations since the latter situation would make it difficult, if not impossible, to fulfill the high calling of being a wife and mother *first*, faithfully serving the home in order to satisfy her divinely sanctioned complementary

1. The "wisdom" argument is perhaps the majority argument among evangelicals. See Kotter, "Does Sarah Palin Present a Dilemma for Complementarians?" for a concise summary and defense of this popular position. See also, Chanski, *Womanly Dominion*.

role (Titus 2:3–5), a role that is just as pleasing and important to God (if not more so) as any form of public service. Nonetheless, a decision of that nature is best left between a couple and the counsel of their elders.

While it is normative that men serve as protectors and national leaders, God has indeed gifted certain women to lead nations (states, cities, towns, communities, etc.), and the chance of a woman running for president or garnering the nomination in this country is real. If God was pleased in times past to raise up gifted women who capably led nations in the past, we can expect God to work similarly in our day to lead us and rule over us on occasion, especially given the abysmal record of men who have failed this nation so greatly on the issues of faith and morals. If the male rulers of this nation are lacking in this commitment to godly rule, then perhaps it is time for another Deborah to be raised up—someone who will force the nation back into submission to God and his precepts. Be that as it may, it should be our hope that God will raise up Christian folks who are committed to upholding biblical principles, including the primary responsibility in the home—whether that person be a male or a female.

Having said that, this understanding of the role of women in civil government does not logically lead to women serving as pastors or elders in churches, nor does it lead to a woman "exercising authority over a man" (as some evangelicals have expressly feared). The kingdom of God and the kingdom of man are two completely different organizations that—while each established by God—were not set up with the same conditions. The former has clear roles and divisions of responsibility delineated for both men and women and must be protected. But since the Bible is silent on the latter, any attempt to transfer the requirements for the church as the binding criteria on secular public servants is asking too much. Let us remember to be firm where Scripture requires us to be but gracious when it does not speak as clearly. Christians tend to get into trouble and cause needless division when they try to go beyond what God has plainly revealed.

7

The Christian's Duty to Civil Government

THE 1999 American comedy film *Office Space* is a satire of work life in a typical white-collar business environment, a veritably bleak work situation in corporate America. The movie focuses on several employees who are "fed up" with the excessive bureaucracy and overregulation of their jobs. Peter, the main character, finally does something about it. He announces that he simply will not work anymore and instead pursues a lifelong goal of "doing nothing." Yet in a twist of irony, despite his best efforts at laziness and insubordination, and the more he does nothing, he is rewarded with a promotion, mostly for his refreshing candor on life.

Many of us can probably sympathize with Peter's comical plight, but the reaction to his situation was far from what the Bible teaches us. In fact, when it comes to the issue of submitting to authority—especially in regard to human government—the apostle Peter introduces the concept that Christians are to submit voluntarily to those in authority (1 Pet 2:13–14). Paul also captures this essence generally in his Titus epistle in which he reminds his readers to be "submissive" and "obedient" (Titus 3:1). But Paul's real discussion of the Christian's duty toward civil government is found in his letter to the Romans. Once Paul brings together the great themes of the Bible—universal sinfulness, the law, judgment, salvation, eternal destiny, faith, works, grace, justification, election, sanctification, the work of Christ, the hope of all believers, the nature and life of the church—he writes about the duties of all Christian citizens.

Beginning in Romans 12, Paul begins his teaching on the idea of being in subjection.[1] Carrying this idea from chapter 12 onward, the apostle teaches that Christians are to be subordinate to God, presenting our bodies "as a living sacrifice, holy and acceptable to God" (Rom 12:1–2); subordinate to the interest of others, because "we, though many, are one body in Christ, and individually members one of another" (Rom 12:3–21); and subordinate to the governing authorities, "for there is no authority except from God, and those that exist have been instituted by God" (Rom 13:1–7).

What ties Paul's message together on the teaching of subordination is fundamental to the area that should exemplify the Christian life—*service*. Service not provided out of a spirit of reluctance or self-interest but by a spirit of true subservience.

Perhaps you heard the story of a man in civilian clothes during the American Revolution who rode past a small group of soldiers repairing a defensive barrier. The leader of the group was shouting orders to the other men but was making no attempt to help them. The rider stopped, dismounted, and asked the solider why he did not help out.

---

1. For a thorough exegesis of Romans 12—13 regarding the issue of subjection, see Deffinbaugh, "The Christian and Civil Government."

"Sir, I am a corporal!" he retorted. The stranger apologized, for he was not aware of the man's rank, and proceeded to assist the weary soldiers in the repairs.

"Mr. Corporal, next time you have a job like this and not enough men to do it, go to your commander-in-chief, and I will come and help you again." The helpful stranger was none other than General George Washington.

The point here is that we cannot truly serve others while at the same time serving ourselves as a priority. The corporal believed himself to be above helping others he outranked militarily—superior to the task—so much so that he refused to lend a helping hand to the weary soldiers. The corporal saw himself as better than the job and those with whom he served. Without the corporal's subordination, the task was doomed. Likewise, without true submission from Christians, charitable service—the kind required by God—is impossible.

Pursuing one's own self-interest above all others makes service to God, family, country, coworkers, and friends unmanageable. The idea that self or *numero uno* comes first might be characteristic of the American way of life, but it is not how the Bible teaches us to live. "No one can serve two masters" (Matt 6:24). Subordination as a mindset and a way of life comes before loving service. This is precisely the point Paul makes to the Philippians when he talks about the voluntary subordination of the Son, "Who being in very nature God, did not consider equality with God something to be used to his own advantage; rather, he made himself nothing by taking the very nature of a servant, being made in human likeness. And being found in appearance as a man, he humbled himself by becoming obedient to death—

even death on a cross" (Phil 2:6–8)! Jesus's life is an example of true subordination, showing us exactly what it takes to truly serve God, government, and man.

SUBMISSION EVEN TO UNGODLY GOVERNMENTS

One of the most contentious debates I witnessed at work (in the wardroom of a navy destroyer) was whether the American colonists were biblically justified in their revolution against King George III. The person arguing against the colonists' actions was woefully outnumbered (in fact, if I recall correctly, he was the only one suggesting this). This individual did raise some interesting points, but the point here is not to argue for or against that instance but to provide some biblical examples that should serve as models to us for how we are to effect change for the good. Let's begin with the Old Testament story of Daniel.

Daniel could have been used as the example for Paul's teaching in Romans 13:1–7 for his gracious attitude and obedience to secular government throughout his entire ordeal (except in two specific instances where Daniel was prohibited from doing something God commanded). You see, Daniel was a political hostage taken captive by King Nebuchadnezzar of Babylon. There was nothing spectacular about Daniel. He had no royal lineage or political clout of which to speak in his homeland, yet his captors came to admire him greatly over time. Kings listened when he spoke.

Why? Why would anyone listen to a lowly Hebrew captive? What could possibly make the great king of

Babylon fall "prostrate before Daniel and pay him honor and order that an offering and incense be presented to him" (Dan 2:46)?

I submit the answer is found in the manner in which Daniel conducted himself. First, Daniel, despite being carried away from his friends, family, and house of worship, served the Babylonian king when he was called upon for help. Even though Daniel, by all human accounts, could have rightly refused to give honor to any captor, he chose to subordinate himself to the pagan, human government of Babylon because Daniel recognized that even the heathen government was divinely ordained. He showed those in authority over him that he respected their position and cooperated and supported the government by being educated in the ways of the Babylonians and working diligently in his studies (Dan 1:1–4). He also sought to interpret the king's dreams and writing on the wall (Dan 2, 4–5) and even spare the lives of others (Dan 9).

Second, not only did Daniel take a stance for divine obedience in submitting to his government, but he also practiced what he preached in disobedience to the authority as well. The first time was in refusing to eat the king's food or the king's wine (Dan 1:8). The second and more well-known case of his civil insubordination was in Daniel's refusal to submit to King Darius's decree that forbid praying to Yahweh. Even though Daniel knew full well the consequences for not obeying, he thought it more important to obey God even though the civil authorities had outlawed the practice.

And for his moral stance—both in obeying and disobeying—the prophet was able to curry favor with the political leaders of his day. Daniel was a man who practiced what he preached. He eagerly cooperated with the governmental system under which God had placed him and only disobeyed and refused to submit in the rare circumstances that the former contradicted the latter.

Then there is the case of John the Baptist. The cousin of Jesus was a man who spoke his mind on morality and the loose morals that characterized the Herodian dynasty, and he refused to back down. While this candor ultimately cost John his head, Herod, the ruler, strangely found himself compelled by John and his teachings. Herod was "exceedingly sorry" (Mark 6:26) when he was tricked by his wife into executing John the Baptist.

One could also point out the perfect life and example of Christ Jesus. He was a man who taught submission to authority, teaching his disciples to give to Caesar all that belonged to him (Mark 12:17) and even refusing to let Peter defend him against the Roman authorities when they came to take his life (Luke 22:47–51; John 18:10). Even in unjust circumstances, Jesus obeyed those appointed over him. Doing this gained the attention of the political leaders who only reluctantly partook in his death.

Even today, it is godly men and women who are subject to the governing authorities, and those whose lives match what they teach are the ones sought out by political figures. Perhaps no other leader of the past century has been sought out by more presidents, heads of states, and leading political figures around the world than the evangelist Billy Graham. I am convinced this is so because more than anything else Mr. Graham could do for those leaders, he lived and taught that we are to be subject to God, to his Word, and to the government under which we are placed.

If Christians want to know how they can make a lasting, impactful change on society, the primary way—the biblical way—is to be obedient to God by being obedient to human government and to serve it joyfully. If we truly render unto Caesar what is owed to him, then we give government our money so they can carry out their tasks, and we give them our honor so they can do their jobs. "There is no authority," Paul reminds us, "except that which God has established" (Rom 13:1). Christians should be careful about complaining about their elected leaders and rebelling against them because doing so "is rebelling against what God has instituted, and those who do so will bring judgment on themselves" (Rom 13:2).

It will take a completely radical revolution to change our current state of affairs, but the only true and lasting revolution for the good of society can come through Christian service to God and to country.

Conclusion

REPUBLICAN PRESIDENTIAL hopeful Rick Santorum is the latest candidate to find himself surrounded by a (trumped-up) controversy for his socially conservative beliefs. It was fairly obvious that Santorum would soon be scrutinized heavily for his so-called extreme views and outrageous statements following his victory in the 2012 Iowa Caucasus. I was curious to discover what caused so many folks to get apoplectic, so in the wake of Santorum's gaining popularity, I decided to *Google* "Outrageous Rick Santorum Statements," and this is what I found. More than four million results returned, with an entire front page listing of an article entitled, "Rick Santorum's Top 10 Most Outrageous Campaign Statements." And sure enough, to no one's surprise, the number-one "most outrageous statement" uttered by Santorum was his vow to "annul all same-sex marriages," arguing that homosexual relationships "destabilize" society.

Outrageous! What gumption!

Or is it?

In fact, Santorum, I believe, is merely following the example of the church throughout the ages, examples set forth in both the Old and New Testament by Christians who have fulfilled their duty to bring their values to the political field. I understand there remains a sense of political agnosticism among people in Christendom—folks who are not convinced the church has any say in the public square or in the political arena. But given the testimony of saints throughout the ages, it is hard to accept this wall-of-separation thinking.

In the Old Testament, for example, we read of Ahab, who used his secular power for selfish reasons, including confiscating personal property, marrying a pagan, and worshiping a false God, doing more "to arouse the anger of the LORD, the God of Israel, than did all the kings of Israel before him" (1 Kgs 16:33). Yet no one spoke out until Elijah risked his life to declare the king unjust. Isaiah was appointed to go to the palace and talk with a number of kings, voicing God's displeasure with the nation. Amos was another prophet who lamented the depravity of the nation and witnessed visions of Israel's destruction as a consequence for their behavior. And for giving voice to heeding morality, each of the prophets faced humiliation, physical danger, and even death.

In the New Testament, we read of John the Baptist, who called attention to the king's immoral choices and was beheaded for it (Matt 14:1–12). Jesus, too, criticized public servants, calling Herod a "fox" (Luke 13:32), a metaphor meaning worthless and sly. And on numerous occasions Jesus rebuked the leaders of Israel, corrected the Sanhedrin, and criticized the leading authorities for how morally bankrupt they actually were.

All of this is not to advocate a Christian theocracy or anything even closely resembling John Calvin's Geneva; quite frankly, I much prefer our form of government over against any humanly instituted theocracy. However, this is simply to point out Christians have a duty to bring their values to the political field. Those Christians who chose to remain on the sidelines and remain absent from the political process have no more reason to be upset than, let's say, would Dr. Frankenstein after his monster terrified the entire town and utterly destroyed it, only to have someone come up to him and ask, "Where did this monster come from?" Like Dr. Frankenstein's tragic reply, Christians are left with a similar answer: "I created it."

Christians have a responsibility when they vote. When they vote, they are casting their "will" or "choice" (from the Latin *votum*). Being granted the opportunity to cast our *will* on society brings with it a tremendous amount of responsibility, for we are called to do the right thing before God. Going to the voting booth and voting is not a license to vote irresponsibly, nor is it liberty for us to vote however we think it will benefit us personally. Our vote is not freedom to impose selfishness on others; rather, it is essential that when a vote is cast, it is a vote for what is pleasing in the sight of God according to his revealed witness and testimony. That is one duty of every Christian citizen in a free and open society—voting for what is right and what is ethical. Our consciences need to be informed by the Word of God, allowing God's testimony to guide us in voicing our will in civil government. Christianity, we need to remember, should not be left outside the voting booth or abandoned in the parking lot, because that's never what our Founding Fathers intended, and that is certainly not what Jesus taught.

I end simply by observing what Samuel Adams, sometimes called the "Father of the American Revolution," signer of the Declaration of Independence, and member of the constitutional convention, said, "I conceive we cannot better express ourselves than by humbly supplicating the Supreme Ruler of the world . . . that the confusions that are and have been among the nations may be overruled by the promoting and speedily bringing in the holy and happy period when the kingdoms of our Lord and Savior Jesus Christ may be everywhere established, and the people willingly bow to the scepter of Him who is the Prince of Peace."[1]

True freedom is being obedient to Christ, and part of that obedience is voting wisely so that we may obtain the "happy period" of which Adams (and certainly others) spoke. It's time we recognize that we are truly a nation "under God," subject to his commands, and responsible for our moral decisions. Lest we succumb to the same fate that befell the nation of Israel repeatedly after their numerous moral collapses, we fulfill our civic duty to stand up for righteousness and safeguard morality when given the chance, and vote with a conscience guided by Scripture to ensure the greatest moral leaders possible are guiding and directing an American society *instituted by God*.

1. Adams, *The Writings of Samuel Adams*, 407.

Bibliography

Adams, Samuel, ed. Harry Alonzo Cushing. *The Writings of Samuel Adams*, vol. 4. New York: G. P. Putnam's Sons, 1908.

Barton, David. "The Separation of Church and State." No pages. Online: http://www.wallbuilders.com/libissuesarticles.asp?id=123.

Beckwith, Francis J. "Is It Permissible for a Christian to Vote for a Mormon?" *Christian Research Journal*, volume 30, number 5 (2007).

———. *Politics for Christians: Statecraft as Soulcraft*. Downers Grove, IL: InterVarsity, 2010.

Black, Amy E. *Beyond Left and Right: Helping Christians Make Sense of American Politics*. Grand Rapids, MI: Baker, 2008.

Bohon, Dave. "Supreme Court Declines Case Banning Crosses on Utah Highways." No pages. Online: http://thenewamerican.com /culture/faith-and-morals/9643-supreme-court-declines-case -banning-crosses-on-utah-highways.

Brachear, Manya A. "Catholic Charities of Rockford Ends Foster Care, Adoption Services." No pages. Online: http://articles. chicagotribune.com/2011-05-26/news/ct-met-rockford -catholic-charities-st20110526_1_catholic-charities-adoption -services-care-and-adoption.

Buchanan, Patrick J. *Suicide of a Superpower: Will America Survive to 2025?*. New York, NY: Thomas Dunne, 2011.

Campolo, Tony. *Red Letter Christians: A Citizen's Guide to Faith & Politics*. Ventura, CA: Regal, 2008.

Chanski, Mark. *Womanly Dominion: More Than A Gentle and Quite Spirit*. Amityville, NY: Calvary, 2008.

Deffinbaugh, Bob. "The Christian and Civil Government (Romans 13:1–7)." No pages. Online: http://bible.org/seriespage/christian -and-civil-government-romans-131-7.

Grudem, Wayne. *Politics According to the Bible: A Comprehensive Resource for Understanding Modern Political Issues in Light of Scripture*. Grand Rapids, MI: Zondervan, 2010.

Hitchens, Christopher and Douglas Wilson. *Is Christianity Good for the World?*. Moscow, ID: Canon, 2009.

Kennedy, D. James, and Jerry Newcombe. *How Would Jesus Vote? A Christian Perspective on the Issues*. Colorado Springs, Co: WaterBrook, 2008.

Kotter, David. "Does Sarah Palin Present a Dilemma for Complementarians?." No pages. Online: http://www.cbmw.org/Blog/Posts/Does-Sarah-Palin-present-a-Dilemma-for-Complementarians-Part-1.

Mendes, Elizabeth. "In U.S., Fear of Big Government at Near-Record Levels." No pages. Online: http://www.gallup.com/poll/151490/fear-big-government-near-record-level.aspx.

Myers, Jeffery L. *Vital Truth: Christian Citizenship*. Nashville, TN: Lifeway, 2003.

Powers, Kirsten. "Mitt Romney's Mormon Problem in the Iowa Caucuses Simply Won't Die." No pages. Online: http://www.thedailybeast.com/articles/2011/12/16/mitt-romney-s-mormon-problem-in-the-iowa-caucuses-simply-won-t-die.html.

Reiter, Mark. "Federal Judge Says Ten Commandments Shall Stay At Courthouse." No pages. Online: http://www.covenantnews.com/newswire/archives/020275.html.

Santarelli, Christopher. "U.S. House Members Banned from Writing 'Merry Christmas' in Official Mail." No pages. Online: http://www.theblaze.com/stories/u-s-house-members-banned-from-writing-merry-christmas-in-official-mail/.

Santorum, Rick. *It Takes a Family: Conservatism and the Common Good*. Wilmington, DE: ISI, 2005.

Sproul, R. C. *Now, That's a Good Question!* Carol Stream, IL: Tyndale House, 1996.

Starnes, Todd. "Federal Judge Prohibits Prayer at Texas Graduation Ceremony." No pages. Online: http://www.foxnews.com/us/2011/06/02/prayer-prohibited-at-graduation-ceremony/.

Thavis, John. "Cardinal Ratzinger Lays Out Principles on Denying Communion, Voting." No pages. Online: http://www .catholicnews.com/data/stories/cns/0403722.htm.

White, James. "An Eye for an Eye? Exodus and Abortion." *Christian Research Journal*, volume 27, number 1 (2004).

Winn, Pete. "Senate Approves Bill that Legalizes Sodomy and Bestiality in U.S. Military." No pages. Online: http://cnsnews.com/news /article/senate-approves-bill-legalizes-sodomy-and-bestiality -us-military.

www.ingramcontent.com/pod-product-compliance
Lightning Source LLC
La Vergne TN
LVHW021621080426
835510LV00019B/2690